THE ROLLER COASTER
– UP N DOWN! –

AN EXTENSION OF THE MICROSCOPE
(SOME CALL IT POETRY)

Anna "Annina" Lorenzi

Original Title:
"The Roller Coaster - Up&Down! - Un'estensione di The Microscope
(qualcuno le chiama poesie)"
Translated from Italian by: Starleen K. Meyer

An "Original A19" Project

Anna "Annina" Lorenzi
www.annina19.com

Reader "Zero": Starleen K. Meyer

Proofreaders: Prof. Gabriella Nisi, Dott. Roberto Lorenzi

Book and cover design: A19
Original cover image by: David Traña
Copyright ©2021 Anna Lorenzi.

ISBN 9798728446248

*Dedicated to those who truly believe in the deep
value of Friendship as a form of Love
and in the immense significance of a Promise.*

*And to all those who, however it turns out,
don't really know how to get down from roller coasters.*

To all of you who find reading me pleasurable.

To those who have always been there for me, and who'll continue to be.
And to those who aren't, anymore.

And to those who, in any case, have had and will always have their "because" in my life.

– INDEX –

This new collection of poetry is for me an extension and natural completion of the preceding one, which came out just a few months ago. It's a kind of "link" between the pre-, post- and (in part) "during" of my life's chapter that was The Microscope. A collection of snapshots immortalized with a pen. An extremely beautiful, intense and stupefying chapter that is finished ... unfortunately. Around it, though, was more than a world. A world worth painting and recounting. I'm happy to share with you this book, with all its honest and sincere spontaneity.

I'll reveal a secret to you, too. The original "Extra Snapshot" of The Microscope, which has never before been published, well, you'll find it among these pages. And it really began with ... "The Roller Coaster..."

Because, maybe, all of us are born with tickets in our pockets for at least one go on the roller coaster, only no one ever knows how long it will last, and what effect it will have. Getting on and trying our best is the only thing we can do. The rest, then, is to be seen. At least, that's what I believe, so...

Enjoy! Up&Down!!!
And live all these "goes".

AI9

II
____

– THE ROLLER COASTER: THE ORIGIN –
(A NON-PREFACE)

uuuuUUP!!!

   ...& down.

It's what you expect, is due...   *destiny.*

  All aboard?!

Journey   *pathway*

   alone

A collection...   *of Life*

   emotions.

Flat, curve *Uphill* *downhilllllll...*

  Dowwwwn!! *Speed* *Fear*

HIGHS *lows* S T A L L E D

  tears... *Smiles* *Screams!*

and then... *memories* *...us (?!)*

No *rules* *Non-Time* *Forever* and Never.

It is what it is: UP!&Down,

  The Roller Coaster.

IV

– SLOW LOOP –
(PRE–THE MICROSCOPE)

Calm

_ F L A T _   Apparent

I *n T e* R *mi* T *te* n t   *Lights*

r   a   z   e

. . .

– LOOP #01 –

"On the edge of pleasure,
on the edge of error..."

Teetering between reason and feelings,
tightrope walkers on a thin thread,
between dream and reality.

A perfect game of equilibrium
at constant risk of falling,
and onto which side no one ever knows.

And yet incapable of stopping the dancing
to the rhythm of one's own heart.
Incapable of stopping the Living.

Maybe...

[Retouched: March 2021.
Original text: from an exchange of "images," January 2003]

– LOOP #02 –

The slow lifting of the fog,
a light breeze moves the tops
of the trees resigned to the fall,
messily, barely caressing them.

The sharp smell of humid earth and of iron, cement,
of trains ready to leave for the sea
or for delirious cities.

The smell of coffee
of a forced reawakening,
of desert paths, abandoned, still for a bit.

An unusual morning.

The dawn has already become day,
intense and dazzling light,
blinding, surprising.

A deep breath,
the memory of a gaze, of a smile,
of a hug…

A happy thought.

Of a soul once again filling up with life,
of a heart still able to be startled.
Of a night without time.

A night unable to be comprehended,
of being grasped, fully understood,
stopped in the immensity of a dream.

Incredibly real and perfect,
in every instant breathed, consumed,
lived…

Finished.

Without a second to ask oneself,
to question oneself, to think,
to doubt.

Overflowing with thoughts,
full of the unexplainable,
of a full, marvelous infinity.

Just an unusual morning…

[Retouched: March 2021; original text: 2006]

– LOOP #03 –

[Retouched: March 2021. Original text: 2006]

Keep me with you, pretty please.

Nothing wrong,
just a hug.

Only an instant extorted from time,
snatched from the whole world,
from everything that we will be, later,
tomorrow.

Only tonight
only a breath of life,
a stolen smile,
a little instant.

Only us, destiny, and nothing else.
The rest will return,
tomorrow…

Only a breath,
only a caress.

Keep me with you, pretty please.

Nothing wrong, my friend,
just Love.

Reflecting...

Mirrors that look at each other, mirrors that speak to
each other,
Mirrors that hate, and mirrors that love.

Fogged up mirrors, glittering mirrors,
mirrors that are full of themselves, and hesitant mirrors.

Dirty mirrors, perfect mirrors,
shiny mirrors, and false mirrors.

Mirrors that smile, scream, cry,
whisper, fight, make up or break.

Mirrors that exchange emotions
among themselves or by themselves,
most of the time, inconclusive reactions.

Mirrors...

Hundreds, millions, billions of mirrors
that project falsified images,
probably already projected by others.

Merely mirrors
that reflect themselves in other mirrors

in a world full of mirrors.

But you, what do you see?
What do you observe?

Do you show yourself, or reflect?
(Or do you maybe succeed in doing both?)

Do you really stand out, are you really you?
Your eyes don't fool me.

(Will we know how to recognize each other if we meet in
the street,
for example, now?)

[March 2019]

I let the messy knot of my thoughts
undo in the wind,

that every fear, uncertainty, might be carried away by it,
kidnapped and dissolved

in the graceful dance of newborn grass
and of vigorous fronds.

I let the tepid embrace of spring's sun
surround me and warm me.

I close my eyes, and listen to that which
the wind knows how to whisper to me in its hisses.

I breathe.
Intensely, delicately.

As if I sensed for the first time those smells
that know how to immediately take my memory
to other times, other places, not far from here.

I breathe deeply,
and I listen.

Every part of me fills up, expands,
at home.

I reopen my eyes, slowly.

In front of me The Mountain.
My mountain and its powerful immensity.

I smile.
Around me no one.

An image goes through me,
touching my soul.

Around me no one,
and yet, you here, next to me,
as always.

What tale do you want to tell me, today?

[April, 2019]

The wind of a storm about to arrive blows,
thunder still in the distance booms muffled,
threatening clouds chase each other in the sky.

The light is ever more weak,
overcome by the gray of the shadows that anticipate
evening.
Windows light up, street lamps go on.

Violently, suddenly, the silence is broken.
"It's the devil playing lawn bowls!"*

Before night falls, it will rain.
Hopefully, not too much.

(And to think that if you were here, now,
you would certainly bring the sun…)

*Italian idiom expressing the booming sound of claps of thunder

[May 2019]

– LOOP #07 –

If you were a flower,
would you ever like to be stepped on?

If you were a tree,
would you ever like to be cut down?

And if you were a dragonfly,
would you ever like someone to pull off your wings?

And if you were a person,
would you ever like to be derided, humiliated, tortured
or killed?

[From the post series "Waiting to meet Laura" -
for the novel Meeting Laura, 2020 - March, 2020]

- LOOP #08 -

Two thin lines dance without stopping
dance to the rhythm of two melodies,
different, but from the same poem.

They dance under the sun, the rain, in a storm,
dance afar, barely brushing each other… instants.
And yet they dance under the same sky, they always have.

They follow their own path, inevitably,
curved, angular, cutting, surprising,
sometimes tangled up, enmeshed,
other times simply straight.

They travel on parallel tracks, distant,
able to intersect each other rapidly,
only for a few seconds, a common destiny.

They travel at two different speeds,
they go far from each other, they go near, they get lost,
they find each other,
they go through each other, they separate only to find
themselves, again,
in a time impossible to define, impossible to get.

Two thin lines dance without stopping,
they dance to the rhythm of primordial drums,
different theater stages, same Life.

*[From the post series "Waiting to meet Laura" -
for the novel* Meeting Laura, *2020 - March, 2020]*

Lights

Bright colors, vivid, shining,
make your smile a perfect smile,
your beauty almost surprising,
the undisputed center of attention, you think.

They cast a spell over the stage's spotlights,
they fascinate and attract with all their brilliance.
It's almost impossible to resist them, to remain in the
shadow,
to stay there only to watch.

It would be so easy to give in to the temptation,
so easy to let oneself be fooled…

(Is that smile of yours really real?)

Reflected lights, lights that deceive.
Lights that exalt that which is to be shown.

Warm lights, golden lights, real lights, and inexistent
lights
that when turned on illuminate only apparent truths.

Lights that reveal a part of you,
only a part of you.

Will you remember not to forget who you were?

Will you remember what your yesterday was?
Will you be able to stay who you are?

And will you still be able to recognize yourself,
tomorrow?

– DEATH-DEFYING LOOP –
(DURING AND AFTER THE MICROSCOPE)

UUUUUP!!!

& Down.

And then… (?)

Suddenly...

everything ON!

again... how come...

Incredulity   *unexpected* gift   *Fear...*

Stupor   *Wonder*   *Joy*

FULL!

"*Word!*"

I like the idea of being born,
so, let there be birth,
The Microscope.

...e r r o r - e m p t i n e s s - n o t h i n g...

Shhh! Silence.

(or almost ...)

Dolcetto o scherzetto?
Trick or treat?

Asked life with a sly air.

Will you leave that kid on your doorstep?
Or will you open up to the one that is ringing the bell?

And what do you perceive in me?
A perfidious smile, or a happy one?

Asked the orange pumpkin in a totally provocative way.

Can you understand what I represent?
Or does your world fool you, and can you barely notice
me?

Am I good or bad?
Do I terrorize or give comfort?

Asked the sheet ghost in its white garb.

In my black eyes, don't you read empathy?
Or are you influenced by your own gaze, so tired by now?

And how do you see me?
Only a pile of bones, or also a heart?

Asked the skeleton hanging in its eternal oscillation.

Don't I have a soul, too, and a contented face?
Or do you only believe that I am the one who scares?

Where, oh where, can hide
genuine Truth?

I'm asking, now, in this crazy reality.

Maybe in the wind's tales
and in its eternal narration.

Or in the spontaneity of a sparrow
and its joyous singing.

Maybe it hides in that immensity
of the highest peak.

In the perfume of the woods
or nature, the wild one.

In the wagging tail of a dog,
it's a little thing, but it's sure.

There's no need to say more,
it's like saying, "I swear."

Maybe it's in the sound of your voice,
in the words that you don't know how to fake.

Or in your spontaneous laugh,
always, impossible to force.

Maybe it's in every phrase
that for a long time I've been writing you.

For good, or bad,
but always Living, though.

And you, do you trust me
and that which I really am?

Do you understand my Nature
and that which I have here, for you, as a gift?

Scrutinize the depths of my Being
and tell me without thinking about it…

do you recognize my "I"
and everything that I have to give?

Can you really sense it,
all my honesty?

And will you always know how to count
on my total devotion?

"*Dolcetto o scherzetto?*
Trick or treat?"

Asked a funny slightly clumsy extraterrestrial.

"Can you leave the exit open ever more wide?"

And with him can you not think of your normality?
Receiving in exchange True Friendship or True Sincerity?

(milk, he likes chocolate a lot, but milk…)

[First original text not used in The Microscope, *"Snapshot n. 18," October 2020]*

– LOOP #11 –

Roller coaster.
Up&Down.

UUUUP!!!

Go up to the highest peak,
and no more emptiness
for fear of a huge crash.

Get up to here, stay on the peak,
the soul is lighter,
there won't be any more crying.

We have seen mountains and enchanted woods,
rivers, lakes, deserts,
and uncontaminated seas.

We have created paintings of all colors,
asking ourselves in the end,
"Is there anything beyond this?"

We have laughed with joy, just like that, all of a sudden,
we have talked for hours,
and have told stories, have explained our truths.

To listen to one another, think, understand, and wait,
to then every time, always,
see us return.

We have looked beyond that which is,
every horizon that is taken for granted, through the fog,
silences,
and scrutinized lots of whys.

We were drenched by the rain, then warmed by the sun;
it was enough to go looking for it
to make it come back.

We have turned on the stars just to make us dream,
and we have held out a hand
just to make us get up, again.

Whether we want to call it chance
or destiny,
we have broken the rules to stay near to each other.

From the shadows to the light, every breath has danced
to the rhythm of a grand heart,
listening to the wind sing.

Close your eyes slowly, and sleep well,
lots of beautiful dreams,
and serene days.

To find ourselves suddenly amazed,
to open the most beautiful gift,
and to uncover ourselves, again, reborn.

To recognize ourselves alike in diversity,
and to choose each other, again, for what we are,
with esteem, respect, and sincere honesty.

To be truly moved, without warning,
by an unexpected gesture, an "I care for you,"
a smile.

To say "sorry," then to be thankful
for every second you've had,
a gesture, a greeting, a word that is Valid.

Then another "Good morning" every morning,
a hug, a thought,
oh, that it could always make itself feel Real.

Months only that seem years,
neither distance nor time exists,
entire centuries, instants.

Existence passes like a snap of fingers,
but thank goodness we are here,
and it's not over, yet.

An incredible departure

for an infinite voyage,
oh, that it could be a new beginning full of Life.

Empty pages and full pages…
pages to fill up with just one goal,
to do best always and only that which comes to us.

It's an incredible story,
still all to be told,
a beautiful road to take, together.

And here's a final snapshot,
which has absolutely nothing to do with endings.

Everything else we'll write,
you and I.

(Word: Thanks)

[First original text for The Microscope, *but not used in it,*
"Final Snapshot," October-November 2020]

It's cold.
It's freezing.

Inside, outside,
around.
Deep inside.

It's a storm.
And snow
that crunches with every step.

The way can't be seen.

Lights off
and dark.
And shadows.

Shadows
of memories
that fill up the brain.

They leave the mind breathless,
and weigh down the heart.

Glass fogged up,
ice, wind that strips away the skin
and the soul.

Slippery steps and precarious balance.

Balance?
What balance?

Truth teetering.
Truth obscured by torment.
Truth damned.

Truth?
Which truth?

The one we want to tell ourselves, maybe.

It's cold.
It's freezing.

Inside, outside,
around.
Deep inside.

Will winter pass?
Will spring come again?

Who knows…
We'll see.

[From the post series: "In one go. Waiting for The Microscope". December 4, 2020]

– LOOP #13 –

Nothingness spreads wide,
drying the earth.

Slowly colors fade;
every leaf falls to the ground.

Death.

Once that recognized profile is seen,
the eye remains ever vigilant.

It perceives the presence,
the soul, now frozen,
still feels Life.

(So much so that it almost bothers it.)

Why do you ignore me?
Asks a shadow from the past.

Because you don't recognize me?
A ray of sunshine asks
reflecting in a dusty mirror.

And yet, we are real and we are here,

heart and reason asking together,
can't you maybe see that which has always been?

Look inside yourself.
Don't you find, maybe, our name, too?

(In the desert, doesn't a flower know how to be reborn?)

A scream rips the night,
breaking the emptiness of the silence.

Everything ends.

Until the dawn of the next day.

[From the post series "In one go. Waiting for The Microscope". December 12, 2020]

I'm everything, I'm nothing.
I'm an idiot,
like hell I am!

I'm the court jester,
I'm the one who gets the blows.
I'm a shield and a defense,
I'm a weapon and an offence.

I'm the refuge in which you can confide,
I'm the fraud from which to escape.
I'm the words you want to hear,
and the discourse you want to avoid.

I'm white, I'm black,
I'm all the colors of the entire world.
I'm truth and then a lie,
I'm the one to send away!

I'm good, I'm bad,
I'm far away, and I'm nearby.
I'm that which is here to have,
and I'm that which you want to hate.

I'm a saint and an assassin,
I'm good and naughty.
I'm gentle and thoughtful,
I'm a shit and also hateful.

I'm a smile, a sincere friend,
I'm the tear of a real crying jag.
I'm the hug that knows how to console,
and I'm that sickness that makes you vomit.

I'm everything or nothing?
I'm an idiot,
and how!

Or, maybe, just a heart
with a soul and a mind…

(from which point-of-view do you want to see your
truth?)

[From the post series "In one go. Waiting for The Microscope". December 16, 2020]

** Translator's note. The original poem relied heavily on rhyming, which is less difficult in Italian than in English, hence, content or rhyming must be sacrificed. Happily, Ms. Lorenzi agreed that in this case the content was more important than the form, and so no effort has been made to reproduce the rhymes in the English translation.*

You are…

A sudden light
that fascinates and muddles,
that reawakens spirit and common sense,
that disturbs them and amazes them.

A cloud on the horizon
before the storm,
a bolt of lightning that blinds,
that disappears, and doesn't stay.

Violent thunder
before the storm,
a strong storm that whistles,
freezes, hurts.

An unexpected storm,
what will it leave?
Death and devastation,
or a better reality?

(Who knows)

You are…

A ray of sunshine

that, rare, surprises.
The smile, the cure
that feeds soul and mind.

Doubts, questions,
joy, emptiness and pain,
truth, certainties,
and maternal love.

A thought that reason
can neither explain, nor say,
but the moon, the sky and the stars
still know how to lie.

An unexpected gift
and that one is certainty.
But of everything that was, now,
is this all that remains?

(And yet, here) you are…

But I'm not writing The Truth,
I'm only tossing around emotions,
I'm playing with words,
sensations and visions.

Is this poetry?
Well, it certainly won't be for you.
And, anyway, what would change

if it were written only for me?

While the hibernating "we" is silent,
and the Id, defenseless,
hidden under the bed,
lies still.

[From the post series "In one go. Waiting for The Microscope". December 20, 2020]

** Translator's note. In accordance with Ms. Lorenzi, the rhyming in the original has had to be sacrificed for content.*

Today
slip slowly, slip again.

On streets, cars, alleys and mansions;
on open umbrellas, dripping street lamps,
on people's heads, and on me.

Today
fall slowly, fall constantly.

Wash away the bad, the emptiness, the freeze, the pain;
then clear the head, soul and heart,
cancel doubt, incomprehension, error.

Today
steal time from us, the one forgotten.

Immobile, to observe you from behind glass,
free your mind of all excesses,
and in a little puddle look at us, reflected.

One day
the rain will eventually end.

In the sky the stars and the moon will reappear,
and the dawn of a new day will know how to bring good
luck.

So, on that future day

I will come to find you.

You will recognize in my glance who I really am,
and in my hug you will still find who I was.

One future day,
when everything will seem better.

When the sun will shine, again, in the sky.

(*"It takes a very rainy day to drown a duck."* – ancient
Chinese saying)

[From the post series "In one go. Waiting for The Microscope". January 2, 2021]

It will be, maybe, one day
a breath of wind.

It will be, maybe, that red leaf
of a maple tree already bare
that falls slowly to the ground.

It will be, maybe, the first fog
of an autumn morning
that wraps around the nearby horizon.

It will be, maybe, the colors of a new canvas,
a perfumed summer dawn,
or a sunset that makes the sky explode.

It will be, maybe, the too noisy silences,
the useless chatter of people,
or some off-key note.

Or it will be, maybe, just an ingenuous word,
pronounced badly,
that will suddenly know how to make you laugh.

It will be, I think, a miniscule detail
to make you think of me, again,
to remind you, suddenly, of who I was.

Who I really am.

Who knows if you will smile,
again.

Or, maybe, it will only take time.
That one without rules, ever.
Least of all for us.

Maybe…
Or maybe not.

I, in the meantime, lay down my arms.
I put down my pen.

Maybe, after all,
I ought to quit
trying to get to you.

[From the post series "In one go. Waiting for The Microscope". January 16, 2021]

And just like that, now annulled.

Oh that your heart might become stone
and your glance ice.

Oh that your soul might shut up
and your Id disappear.

Forever.

Like water that flows,
let everything simply go.

Like an autumn leaf,
resign yourself to the wind, alone.

Resign yourself to death.
Inevitable.

And so you'll stop suffering.

(But is this really the way?)

[From the post series "In one go. Waiting for The Microscope". January 27, 2021]

– LOOP #19! –

Rewind.

Shhh, don't say anything, don't express anything, you
can't.
Disappear.

And yet, I seem to still hear
the sound of your voice,
the sound of those words, your words
still echoing in my mind.

They echo, they worm their way in, they insist.
A sweet melody
or a menacing prophesy.

Far away, far far away, I don't hear them anymore,
dissolved in time that passes…

But no.
They're here.

Shhh, don't say anything,
you can't.

Rewind.
Rewind the tape.

Hide it forever
in your inner labyrinth.

And forget him.

(At least for now…)

52

[From the post series "In one go. In the style of The Microscope". February 3, 2021]

[February 4, 2021]

Topsy-turvy.

Everything upside down, backwards, turned inside out.
Wrong.

If they were falsehoods,
lie to me, again.

If they were lies,
don't ever stop repeating them to me.

(Anyway, what good is truth
if it's so easily confused?)

If those were caresses,
I want your punches straight to the gut back.

And if this were the cure,
I want to catch the disease of you, again.

Because we'll continue, yes, to watch
dawns, sunsets, days and lives pass,
stars that pulse and distant planets shine.

Only, everything was decidedly better…
Together

- LOOP #21 -

Drops.
Drops, fine, fall.

The lake in summer.

My body floats…just,
it's heavy.

Not like the thought of an error, though.

Lying on the rocking of the waves,
head under,

I don't hear anything anymore.

Everything is woolly,
the world doesn't exist anymore.

Distant universes.

And yet, so close…
Close enough to still brush by.

So much so that I seem to exist, still.

But under water, thoughts disappear,
even memories disappear.

And even you.

Even those splendid times that were.
Even the hurt that you still do to me.

And what if I never re-emerged?

56

[February 2021]

The fog dissolves slowly
one cold morning.

Slowly reappearing are the colors
of a winter destined to finish.

While the memory of you, too,
seems to vanish…

Ephemeral illusions.

[February 16, 2021]

– LOOP #23 –

Mud
drips slowly,
it insinuates itself, covers,
wraps.

It dirties the water
as it goes through
even the most limpid,
the most crystalline.

Without pity
drowns
in this way even that being
now destined to disappear.

Someone is talking about a summer rain.
It will wash everything,
they say.

[February 27, 2021
From the post series "In one go. In the style of The Microscope… waiting for TRC!"]

— LOOP #24 —

The azalea won't amaze anymore
with its surprising
cascade of flowers.

The little cherry tree
with its delicate white petals
won't bloom anymore.

No spring for them,
no reawakening.
The freeze killed them.

No treatment will help.
Too late.

Lost forever.
Dead.
Lamented.

Could it have been possible
to think about it before?

[March 1, 2021]

– LOOP #25 –

I raised my gaze,
through the weave of branches close to blooming,
past bothersome street lamps and lit windows,

until I could make out a little star,
right there, not very far
from the timid slice of the moon.

Who knows if you are looking at it, too,
I thought.

[March 1, 2021]

Too much rain has fallen
in one sole place.

Right there, where
a beautiful flower
was about to bloom.

Too bad.

Who knows if ever
that blue of the sky
will return.

Who knows if, one day,
that surprising rainbow
will appear, again.

Who knows if…
ever…

[March 6, 2021]

– LOOP #27 –

You scraped deeply, deeply,
into that bark
that you had lovingly nourished.

It seemed to bleed.
And then… an indelible scar.

And yet that tree
is always there.

Ready to shelter you
from the rain and from the sun.

And to give you a break
just when you want it.

It's in its Nature.

[March 7, 2021]

Words, words, words, words, words…
Thrown to the wind? Really?

To tell, to listen, to make a mistake, to think, to
understand.
Who? Everything and its exact opposite.

- A gagged scream –

Where is all that goodness, all that respect,
and all that esteem?

ON/OFF.

It's so simple, no?
It's enough to pull the plug!

My loss, your gain. Let it be so!
Damned is he who doesn't understand.

Words, words, words, words, words
promised and still more words.

And yet, that for which I swore an oath
I always carry in my heart.

(What an idiot, huh?)

And yet, I'm sorry, that which is Real

can't really ever be erased.

Not even if a thousand and more times
you lied, swearing an oath to God,

that what's been said has been said,
and that this is really a "goodbye."

[March 8, 2021]

On a calm day,
during a night like this,
I will close my eyes, slowly.

A happy thought
will be born all by itself, and, escaping from my hands,
will take flight.

It will rise high, free,
above the buildings and above the sky.

It will go beyond everything,
light and calm.

It will get to you
without ever disturbing,
just to whisper to you,

"Please, be OK
and don't worry…."

It will then explore galaxies,
constellations, and planets,

entire universes never before discovered,
hidden, secret.

And before coming back,
it will steal a star for you

from among them all, for sure, the most beautiful.

Once again it'll go around the world,
and, cautiously,
shhh, shhh, it will bring it to you

because, with it by your side,
oh, that could forever disappear from you
every form of evil.

So that you can feel
your being free, light, full, and happy,

without the weight ever again
of any constriction or scar.

So that you might know how to recognize
truth from lies

and have a loyal Friend next to you,
of the kind that you can always depend on.

So that you can always find the right words, and
that you always know how to get across to those you love.

And finally, because
without a doubt that you might know

that with it nearby, if you want,
you can always smile, laugh, and dream.

But rest well, now, don't think,
Oh, that tomorrow could be for you
a spectacular day.

Of the kind that the heart still knows how to fill,
of the kind that still knows how to bring joy to your soul.

On a calm day,
during a night like this,
I will close my eyes, slowly.

A happy thought
will be born all by itself, and, escaping from my hands,
will take flight…

On a day like these…
when my heart, still beating,
won't feel abandoned, or alone.

[March 9, 2021]

The Roller Coaster,

my loop continues.
In my pocket, a ticket

with no expiration date
opportune

And *again,* may it happen!

- I would like *only to know* *you*
are *happier* *than before. -*

We will see each other, *again,*
beyond *the next* curve

...maybe. (?)

In the meantime, Happy Life always,
I toast you, and
Good Luck.

To all those to whom this collection is dedicated and to those who, in one way or another, for one reason or another, have contributed to its realization.

You'll always have my "thanks."

(And, yes, a little bit to me, too, which I never say.)

Until next time!
AI9

Born in Milan on a rainy Monday morning the 26th of October, 1981. She went to - or, better yet, "went to" - two years of classical studies high school, followed by four years of artistic studies high school, without, in any event, being able to resist dedicating herself to her passions: writing, music, photography, her beloved dogs, engines, travelling and nature. Talking about work, she really does "a little bit of everything," so much so that, together with some friends, she founded a company in Texas that deals with classic cars. Participating in writing contests and working with some Italian magazines, she has published various short stories and articles. Currently, she shares her creative writing accompanied by photographs and images on her personal site, *Diciannove - Prima di nascere ero sull'astronave che aspettavo di scendere* (annina19.com - *Nineteen - Before I was born I was on a space ship waiting to come down*). She is also promoting *The Microscope*, internationally, as well as writing a sequel to her novel, *Meeting Laura*. Both titles are available in English and Italian in all Amazon stores.

— INFO ON THE CITED TEXTS —

Books:

The Microscope. A collection of snapshots immortalized with a pen, by Anna "Annina" Lorenzi, independently published; translated from Italian by Starleen K. Meyer, February 2021. Original Title: *The Microscope. Una raccolta di scatti immortalati con la penna*

Meeting Laura. A novel loosely and partially inspired by the life of… , by Anna "Annina" Lorenzi, independently published; translated from Italian by Starleen K. Meyer, May 2020. Original Title: *Incontrando Laura. Un romanzo liberamente e in parte ispirato alla vita di…*

Blog posts: from annina19.com

The books of the author are available in Italian and English editions, in paperback and eBook formats, on all the Amazon stores.